PATHWAYS

Spiritual Enrichment and Mentorship for

At-risk Adolescent Boys

and Young Adult Men

Written by

Rev. Dr. Andre J. Lewis

Edited by Krystal Berry

©2020 Andre J. Lewis. All Rights Reserved.

ISBN: 978-0-578-67505-3

No part of this book may be reproduced,
stored in a retrieval system, or transmitted by any
means without the written permission of the author.

To my wife and children, who have been a constant support, and who have always allowed me the time necessary to pursue excellence in ministry.

Acknowledgements

I wish to express my gratitude to my family, Dr. T.R. Williams, Dr. Chad Rankin, and my New Faith Church Family…

And of course, to my friends for their spiritual and academic contributions during the research and preparation of this book…

Thank you.

Contents

FOREWORD

When one has lived an experience existentially, it provides a deeper and more enriched understanding of that particular plight. Many seek to give an interpretation of a given situation from a vantage point of distance without ever actually being touched or affected by that in which they determine to analyze. Such is not the case of Dr. Andre Jermaine Lewis. His life's story gives a corollary that is filled with pain and peace, gloom and glory, tragedy and triumph. It is his reality that makes this written work so authentic, authoritative and powerful.

Born in the U.S. Virgin Islands, St. Thomas, and later growing up in the gang festered streets of Boston, eventually Houston, TX gave Dr. Lewis a bird's eye view of the plight of young African American males. His experiences, on the city park basketball courts in Houston at the late of nights and the peeking of the mornings, put him right in the risk of danger and the gathering of knowledge. It was his dichotomous lifestyle as a high schooler, scholar and "rascal" that compelled him to pursue social and spiritual remedies to combat the negative trajectory of his young brothers with whom he dealt daily. He refused to succumb to the fate rendered by societal statistics.

Upon accepting his call into the Gospel ministry, Dr. Lewis' heart was filled with compassion toward the plight of the young African American male. He made, as I once preached, "…his old friends his new assignment." Even before entering seminary, his educational training, and endeavors, both nationally and internationally, were focused on youth and young adult ministries. He delved into the ministry of missions in the USA, Jamaica and Mexico.

It was my privilege to encounter Dr. Lewis in the gymnasium at the New Faith Church in Houston, Texas where I served as Senior Pastor. He was a high school student and had not, at that time, entered the Gospel Ministry. I was really impressed with his wit, personality, and his manners. I later learned that he was in ministry and knew that we had to have him serve on our ministry team; what a ministerial enhancement. His dedication to the way churches should approach Youth and Young Adult ministry was spiritually transforming and culturally relevant. The results of his methods were extremely productive.

Serving now as the Senior Pastor of the New Faith Church in Houston, Texas, Dr. Lewis shares, in this publication, his wealth of knowledge and years of experience in the area of ministry to young African American males. It is an exhaustive work filled with both quantitative data and qualitative experiences which lift us from a state of fatalism to a platform of hope. Pastors and Church leaders will be hard pressed to read this work and not be moved to feel the burden and need to engage in ministry to the Young African American Male.

T. R. Williams, Sr., D.Min.

New Faith Church

Founder/Pastor Emeritus

Houston, Texas

FOREWORD

In a world of confusion and hopelessness, many within the African American community of churches, fraternities, and urban schools, all across this country, have made efforts to generate authentic and relevant strategies that address the reality of losing a generation of African American males to the social ills of our society. With the negative impact of black-on-black crime, drugs, gangs, lack of education, family support structure, mental health issues, mass incarceration, and absence of an affiliation with God, it can be overwhelming for any entity to address. However, Dr. Lewis and the New Faith Church have accepted the challenge by providing a Biblical model of proven ministry strategies to address the spiritual and social ills of young black males between the ages of eighteen to twenty-five. The daunting task of providing hope where there is no hope, love where there is no love, faith where there is no faith is remarkable but for some impossible.

> However, Jesus says … "All things are possible to him who believes." (Mark 9:23 NASB).

The foundation of Dr. Lewis' strategy, in meeting the needs and bearing the burdens of young black males, is rooted in the authority of the word of God. Transformation of the mind, heart, and soul, of any individual, must begin with the Gospel message of Jesus Christ. Moreover, Scripture does provide the knowledge for spiritual growth so that these young men can obtain their identity in Christ rather than the ills of the streets. Additionally, teaching through the Scriptures to address relevant issues helps foster authentic relationships between the mentees and mentors so that communication, accountability, and genuine love is cultivated in a small group setting.

Still, Dr. Lewis' biblical and cultural worldview caused him to think outside of the box with "Pass the Rock" to approach the ministry efforts using what will appeal to these young black males. Therefore, Dr. Lewis' ability to be culturally relevant in accomplishing spiritual and psychological transformation, with a biblical foundation as a model, can be transported to all churches that sense the call of ministry in meeting the needs of young black males. These ministry strategies provided by Dr. Lewis create a path of ratifying delinquency among young black males.

Therefore, our communities can be encouraged for the future of our African American churches and communities because of the investment our churches make now in our young black males.

Chad E. Rankin, DMin.

PATHWAYS

Chapter One:
Starting at Rock Bottom

The summer months, in Houston, TX, have always proven to be quite eventful for families. The announcement of music concerts, Broadway shows, crawfish festivals and hundreds of thousands of celebrations in the city are all a part of the Houston summer culture. But for one family, during the summer months of May 2012, the beginning of the summer would prove to be a much more disturbing and despairing experience. A young black man and several of his friends, all of whom were considered gang members of a local group in a neighboring city of Houston, committed a heinous crime. The young man, who at the time was a basketball player for a small junior college in Texas, was home on leave. He was removed from the basketball team indefinitely for participating in illegal activities that were detrimental to his teammates.

Immediately after his dismissal, his aunt, contacted his youth pastor, from Bethany Church, to meet her at a local restaurant. At the dinner meeting, the young man appeared with his aunt and he was quite belligerent. It was apparent that he didn't want to be there at all, but she was clearly campaigning to save his life. She began to share how he had been removed from the team for selling marijuana and participating in gang activity. With tears in her eyes, she was emotional. She was hurt.

But the young man was unmoved.

Throughout the conversation, there was no question that he was possibly at that meeting under the influence of something and in a very abrupt manner, the young man got up from the table and walked outside stating he was ready to go. Seeing the aunt visibly upset with his behavior and desperate for help for her nephew, the youth pastor prayed in the midst of the situation and the meeting ended.

In the same weekend, and with no impression made on the young man, he and four friends rode to the parking lot of a local restaurant to make a drug deal. As in many instances, the drug deal went bad. That was all it took for gunfire to erupt and the end result was one person who lay dead while another was severely injured. Systematically and by Texas law, everyone involved was arrested and that included the young man from dinner. Later that night, his aunt called, her voice riddled with tears and sadness, to notify the youth pastor that her nephew had been charged with attempted murder and homicide.

For the next year, the young man would spend every day and night in jail awaiting trial.

During a pastoral visit to the jail, from his church, the young man showed no remorse and articulated that he was not remorseful for what he did. His excuse was he found it necessary to protect his family—the gang. This was a young man who matriculated from a prominent high school, who lived in a lavish home, his uncle was a retired and successful corporate executive, and his aunt a full-time parent and support system. This just did not make sense. *How could this have happened to someone who seemingly had it all*?

On the day of sentencing, the church went into prayer for the young man and his family. There was great mourning within the church and community because this kid was quite likable and impressionable. His basketball prowess and versatility on the court were amazing—he had single-handedly taken his high school basketball team to a state championship game during his senior year. He was an active Sunday school, youth church, and Bible study participant. With all of these wonderful credentials and affiliations, the church still found itself in prayer for a favoring outcome for such a talented but troubled young soul. *How did this happen? Why did it happen?* It seemed readily apparent that somehow his community, his family, and his church *failed* this young man.

The truth was that there was nowhere for the young man to turn to after high school. Unplanned summer months, after graduation, were filled with temptations that led to trouble for young black boys and men in the area, and there was no outlet for him after graduation. Another reality was that Bethany Church did not have a relevant or functional ministry to deal with the issues of the culture that confronts young black males on a daily basis. The support of the youth ministry was now out of reach because of age and interests, and the young man was left to navigate life on his own. Searching for significance caused him to fall prey to the allure of gangs and a street life from the dorms of college life.

Tragically, this young man is only one of hundreds of thousands in our nation whose story mirrors that of many of his peers today. This young man grew up in a Christian home with two good role models. He was not a social misfit, and he had the comforts of a nurturing family from an early age. Although he had all of the fringe benefits of his aunt and uncle, there was a void that existed with the absence of his mother; she, who was in and out of his life from birth, struggled with drug addiction. And never knowing his biological father caused him great anguish and grief. Though his aunt was certainly a surrogate mother, she could never replace the presence of his mother in his life. His uncle too was the only man he ever knew as father, but even that had not met the longing he had to know his real father.

The young man's tragedy was a result of not having an outlet where he could express himself or a venue in which he could safely explore manhood and the meaning of family. Even though he had resources and an abundance of material possessions, he lacked connectivity with his family. Always feeling like an outsider, he never embraced even his ample house as a home. For him, as well as many of his counterparts, gang life was the closest option available to them. In a gang, he felt a sense of liberation without judgment and a close family bond. The gang became his community, and it also became the place he protected most violently even at the expense of another's life and his freedom.

Eventually the young man was convicted and sentenced for his role in the bad drug deal. Soon, the quintessential question became, *how could Bethany Church meet the many needs of the youth in this congregation and community that have similar stories like his?* And in that moment, the truth was that the leadership could not answer the question or even devise a plan to meet the needs of the remaining young men in the congregation. The seriousness of the young man's plight arrested the attention of the leadership at Bethany Church and revealed the lack of ministry structure to manage the pain of African American males eighteen to twenty-five.

Eventually, in the wake of the young man's incarceration, many of the young men, within the congregation and city, saw his tragedy as a wake-up call and began to question their futures--some even began to view their relationship with Christ negatively. Many expressed a sense of hopelessness as a reason for the young man's frustrations with life and subsequent incarceration; it was a hopelessness that they admitted that they too felt within themselves at times.

This tragedy revealed many things to the leadership and constituents of Bethany Church and the communities surrounding it. Knowing my expertise and study, they reached out to me to assist them in developing a proactive approach to the issue. The first perspective was that exploring the plight of African American males, eighteen to twenty-five, and their struggle to exist in a pluralistic society is necessary for the church to have an impact on its ministries that cater to adolescent boys and young men. It is also key to what will be thriving men who will make a huge impact on their families and their communities.

What also came to mind, after listening to the hopelessness of these young men, was *what's the church's role in addressing their issues?* Perhaps it would encourage them to return to the church. But this would prove to be a challenge for us. We realized that getting these young men to return to a place of salvific and holistic spirituality would require a ministry model that would meet their needs. This challenge became the focus for developing a model of ministry for African American males eighteen to twenty-five.

As I proceed to provide spiritual insight and practical instructions for changing this narrative of our young black men, I pray that you, in the context of your churches and communities, can 1- gain an understanding of the problem within the church's setting, which may consist of a lack of ministry programs, for African American males, that promotes spiritual growth, reconnection to the church and positive contributions to society, and 2-understand the importance of data and documentation of information that will help you, your ministry leaders and parishioners alike.

Identifying the church as the body to lead this charge was imperative; it is what we have been called to do as disciples of Christ. Because we have an opportunity to cause change, illuminating how young black males are in a desperate struggle for survival reveals that the church must remain diligent as it seeks new and radical ways to successfully confront their demise. The Bethany Church believed it could be done and the "Pass the Rock" ministry was established and implemented. And I believe you can get it done for your church and your community. It is my goal that you will see the importance of addressing the problem that may exist among the young men of your congregations, allow the data within your church and communities to assist you, and allow the gospel of Jesus Christ to aide you in reaching our young boys and men as we accept the church's responsibility in helping to facilitate an effective environment to encourage and guide this special group.

Chapter Two:
Between a Rock and a Hard Place

During my time as a youth minister, I recall talking to a group of young men in the neighborhood about choices and consequences. At the time, two out of the four were expecting to be new fathers. As a result of a series of bad choices, they had not attained gainful employment-- no job, no viable skills, and no diplomas. These young men, like so many in this demographic, were between a *rock and a hard place.* Their life choices, due to a lack of real mentorship and spirituality made them feel like their only alternative was to get fast money through illegal means. The dilemma these young men faced was very real and it becomes the driving force for delinquency in our communities. Far too many times this narrative is reoccurring daily-- not only at a state level but in our country as a whole.

Throughout America, concerns surrounding the negative connotations of African American males from the ages of eighteen to twenty-five remain at the top of societal ills. African American males in this demographic often receive second-class citizenship due to issues of discrimination, a lack of education, joblessness, and a lack of spiritual connectivity to God. Young men, within this age bracket and ethnicity, are often regarded as worthless, dangerous, and unintelligent. In a culture that rewards or even pays tribute to individuals who are proficient, progressive, and educated, more African American males do not view themselves as equivalents but rather derelicts of society. Due to a lack of education, joblessness, and being disconnected from their families, many males within this demographic are labeled by others and label themselves as insignificant.

The labeling that exists within the culture, directed towards black males, is a result of three hundred years of deprivation, denial, discrimination, and lack of equal opportunities. The gross biases within American culture have often led to the persecution of this group, which in many cases has made the victims predisposed to unfair treatment. For many black males, there is a glass ceiling, within the culture, when compared with their white counterparts. The unequal standards that exist between young blacks and young whites are appalling and essentially disturbing. Depraved and dishonest motives are accredited to young African American males who demonstrate the same types of behaviors for which Anglo males are acquitted, disregarded, exempted, or easily pardoned.

In addition to the social plight of young African American males, a spiritual degeneracy has subjugated this group. Spirituality has been a foundation for African American families since early slavery times and was passed down from generation to generation. A relationship with God, amidst centuries of oppression, has been a place of succor and strength for black people. Yet, in this new age of social media, hip-hop music, professional athletes, and the internet, young blacks increasingly see less of a need for a spiritual connection to God or the church.

Instead, the desire to attain status and prominence, hastily and by any means necessary, dictates their rationale. The spiritual compass of young black males remains skewed and is often exchanged for carnal yearnings, which today's culture all-too-readily propagates.

Let us examine the role of the church in all of this too: The Black Church specifically. The Black Church is not blameless of the dejection or concerns surrounding young black males in this country. The message, mission, and ministry of the church has lacked in recent years concerning young black males, and unfortunately few churches have effective plans being executed that focus on their spiritual demise. Some programs that exist lack the contemporary appeal needed to attract and address the concerns of today's young black male. In fact, many programs are antediluvian in their viewpoints and uninformed regarding this group. In other cases, the church has become uninterested in developing adequate programs that foster spiritual development of young black males and nurturing significant male mentoring relationships. Due to the shortage of operative spiritual programs, antiquated messages, and no tangible plan for nurturing spiritual development of young black males, this group has experienced a rapid decline in the culture and religious assemblies.

This demographic has developed a model for life that comes from their distorted environments, which influences the young men to have no affiliation with God. Their moral compasses are damaged because their lifestyles perpetuate a "survival of the fittest" perspective. Religion is not viewed as a means of hope but rather a means of judgment. Survival drives their desires to live, and religion impedes their methods of providing for themselves, which often leads to crime. Many people struggle with the question *"If God is so good, why are things so bad?"* Unfortunately, the sovereignty of God is not considered in the evaluation of their lives apart from God. Instead, oppression and struggle push them further down the rabbit hole and further away from a loving relationship with God.

It is believed that there is an intricate connection between the social abandonment, self-destruction, decline, and disinterest in African American males eighteen to twenty-five and their spiritual depravity. For this reason, the dilemma regarding African American males of this demographic, I believe, must be addressed by the church-- specifically to promote reconnection to church, spiritual growth, and positive contributions to society. And to do this, the church must embrace the spiritual foundations of which it stands on and take an additional personal interest in assisting our young black boys and men through understanding the importance and impact of data relative to those we serve and desire to help.

But what significance does data serve in helping to change this narrative among young black men? Well, understanding how the social demise of African American males is exceptionally disproportioned from their white counterparts, for both minor and more severe crimes, is key to influencing their forward movement. The examination of the immense incarceration rates of young black males identified a key reason for the absence of black males eighteen to twenty-five as productive members of both the black community and The Black Church.

Largely in part to high incarceration rates, many young black males lack formal education, which has prompted a large number of black males to be functioning illiterates who fail at every endeavor to find gainful employment and thus lack the resources to provide for self and family. Lack of education has also proven to increase the rate of crime within communities and intensify the delinquency of males who abandon their families. Unable to find gainful employment, in an economy that demands a high school diploma or GED equivalent, to attain a job, creates further exclusion of young black males. Research affirms that lack of education perpetuates crime and promotes division among young blacks and their families. Law breaking becomes the activity of choice due to the feeling of hopelessness that these young men endure, which increases the level of all types and levels crimes committed among young black males. Tragically, the end result is that many males, within this age group, turn out to be some of the worst offenders within the penal system. All of these dynamics further increase the lack of commitment by young black males to family, church, and community. The research found also displays how a lack of education critically increases delinquency and criminal offenses, including violent crimes.

Further theoretical research validated joblessness as another cause for the demise of young black males in the United States.

Research indicates, in America, the number of jobless black youth is double in comparison to other ethnicities. More black youth are without employment; this creates more idle time and further fragments them from society. No job, lack of formal education, and living with the likelihood of incarceration produces a greater sense of hopelessness among these young men which then motivates them to participate in illegal activities to feel self-worth. Terms like "street-credit" dominate their thinking, especially when they do not feel accepted in society, their own communities and homes and even more sadly the church. The truth is a lack of real mentorship or any real leadership in their lives motivates them to accept street life and street reputations as opposed to being positive contributors of society.

In my research, the issue of hopelessness and its effects were evaluated from a theoretical perspective. It highlighted that many view the church as a place of judgment rather than redemption. For various reasons, the church has not adequately prepared to engage this culture of young men. And the appeal of the culture such as sports, quick money schemes, and illegal activity, has blinded many to a much greater problem that they face, which is a lack of love for God.

I want to suggest to you that being led by the biblical teachings of Christ, collecting and analyzing available data, and using small group ministry within the New Testament church today can help to address the needs of young black males by promoting teaching, worship, and training. The model for this is evident in Jesus' calling of the four fishermen and even the disciples. The New Testament small group model was used in conjunction with developing community among the young men. Research suggested that developing small group establishes community and endorses honest sharing, accountability, mentorship, spiritual growth, and mutual love and respect. In the context of small groups, "Pass the Rock" explored how a small group setting created a new community of faith among the participants' peers.

The aforementioned young man's example is one we wish to avoid in other young black adolescent males and black men. The proactive approach the Bethany Church took to positively influence those young males in and around the church community was not a quick fix, Still, it was done with much caution and in much prayer. I now offer this data and information to you that you may help establish and implement the change that our communities need.

I now "pass the rock" to you.

Chapter Three:
Rock Solid Evidence

What we all must consider is the importance of data when trying to help church constituents. Data assists us with helping those in need within our congregations and communities. Using data has several advantages that include: allowing for strategic approaches to concerns within your congregation, keeping track of information used in ministry, making informed decisions that allow you to make the best choice-- not simply for one individual but for the community as a whole, and it will allow you to solicit the proper resources for enhancing the lives of those you serve. The truth is the statistics on our young black boys and men has not always been great. My time in research gave startling data, but it is this same data that was necessary for considering and implementing a plan that could change this group of young black boys and men. For the purposes of this book, we will look at the data provided for a particular time to see how using this information helped to assist us in guiding the pilot group of young boys and men for the program being recommended. Surely, it will be necessary to look at the current context and capture its data for those you now serve.

In my original research, there were several factors to consider when attempting to assist the young black boys and black men of the Bethany Church. The first factor was that high incarceration rates have led to the demise of young black males within the church and community for the last fifty years. The chart listed below highlights earlier studies found that the rate of delinquency among black youth has increased from 19.6 percent of all juvenile arrests in 1960 to 23.2 percent in 1985.

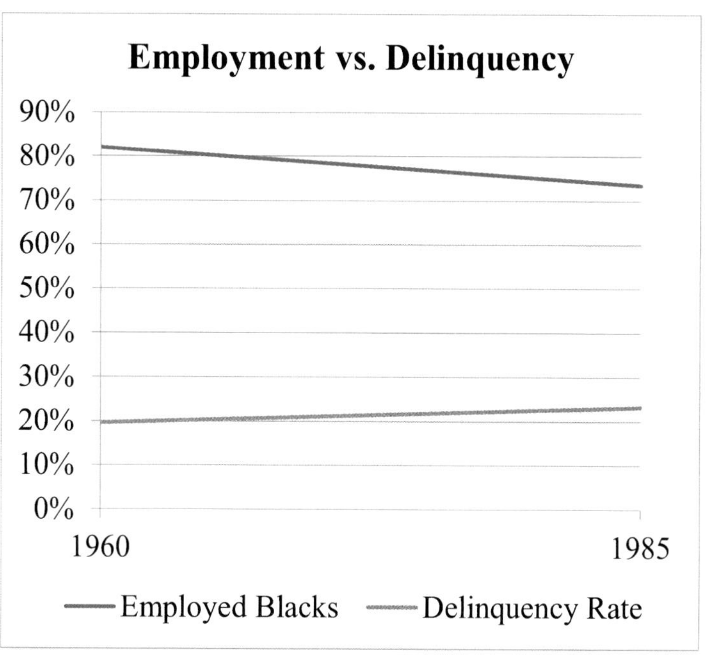

Approximately seven percent of all black adolescents in the ten to nineteen-year-old age group were arrested in 1985.[1] Black youth are arrested more frequently than whites for robbery, rape, homicide, and aggravated assault, according to recent reports.[2]

1. Jewelle Taylor Gibbs, *Young Black and Male in America* (New York: Auburn House Publishing, 1988), 8.

2. Gibbs, *Young Black and Male in America*, 8.

Whites are "the majority of the population and commit crimes at comparable rates to that of people of color," yet people of color constitute sixty percent of the population in prison.[3] In another illustration, one in nine black men between the ages of twenty and thirty-four are in prison.[4] And those numbers, in the context of those I served, were on the rise.

There was then the reality that delinquency was accompanied with joblessness. Joblessness within the black community also affects young black males from uniting with their families and communities. The joblessness among African American males in this study displays a pattern for delinquency that heightens the incarceration rate and absence of males from the community and church. In 1998, blacks participated in the labor force at a rate of 69.9 percent, with 75.0 percent of whites working and 79.8 percent of Hispanics.[5] The unemployment rate among black youth was 24.8 percent, more than twice the rate of white youth at 12.2 percent in July 2014 among all teenagers.[6] These

---

3. Lise Olson, "Give 'Em Hell: Resistance against Racist Oppression in the United States," Reducing the Racial Disparities in Incarceration, WordPress Blog, entry posted September 2007, accessed Oct. 11, 2014, http://antiracistresistance.wordpress.com/reducing-racial-disparities-in-incarceration/.

4. Ibid.

5. United States Department of Labor, "Employment and Unemployment Among Youth Summary," *Economic News Release* (Aug. 13, 2014), accessed May 26, 2015, http://www.bls.gov/news.release/youth.nr0.htm.

6. Ibid.

numbers reflect the lack of participation in black youth regarding the labor force. Joblessness added to the number of crimes of all types including those considered.

What is more is that unemployed black males generally drop out of the job market at increasingly high rates due to discouragement and then turn to a perpetual life of crime. More than one out of five black youth ages eighteen to twenty-one lacks a high school diploma or GED equivalent to attain basic skillsets for an entry-level position or even an apprenticeship. Workers without the requisite education and skills are increasingly left out of the knowledge economy and consigned to poorly paid, dead-end, service sector jobs, which offer few benefits, low job security, and little opportunity for advancement through on-the-job training.[7] Lack of education among young blacks increases the chasm and further distorts their view regarding life in general.

Surely, where there is a lack of education, the data proves that a growth in crime is a result. Nationally, black youth and young adults top the charts in criminal activity in the U.S. Recent polls suggest that the trends of black-on-black crimes are close in comparison to surveys of early 1980s. According to the U.S.

---

7. Stephen L. Klineberg, Jie Wu, and Kiara Douds. *The 2012 Houston Education Survey: Public Perceptions in a Critical Time* (Houston: Kinder Institute for Urban Research, 2013).

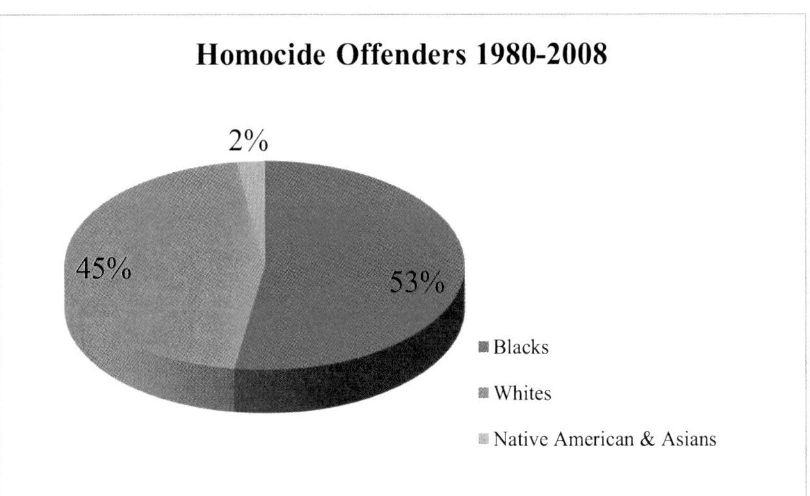

According to the Department of Justice, blacks accounted for 52.5 percent of homicide offenders from 1980 to 2008, with whites at 45.3 percent, and Native Americans and Asians 2.2 percent (see Figure 2). The offending rate for blacks was almost eight percent higher than whites, and the victim rate was six percent higher.[8] Most murders were interracial, with eighty-four percent of white homicide victims murdered by whites, and ninety-three percent of black victims murdered by blacks.[9] According to the FBI Uniform Crime Reports for 2008, black youths, who make up just sixteen percent of the youth population, accounted for fifty-two percent of juvenile violent crime arrests, including 58.5

8. Alexia Cooper, "Homicide Trends in the United States, 1980-2008," National Criminal Justice Reference Service (Nov. 1, 2011), accessed May 20, 2015, http://ncjrs.gov/.

9. Ibid.

percent of youth arrests for homicide and sixty-seven percent for robbery (see Figure 3). Black youths were overrepresented in all offense categories except DUI, liquor laws, and drunkenness.[10]

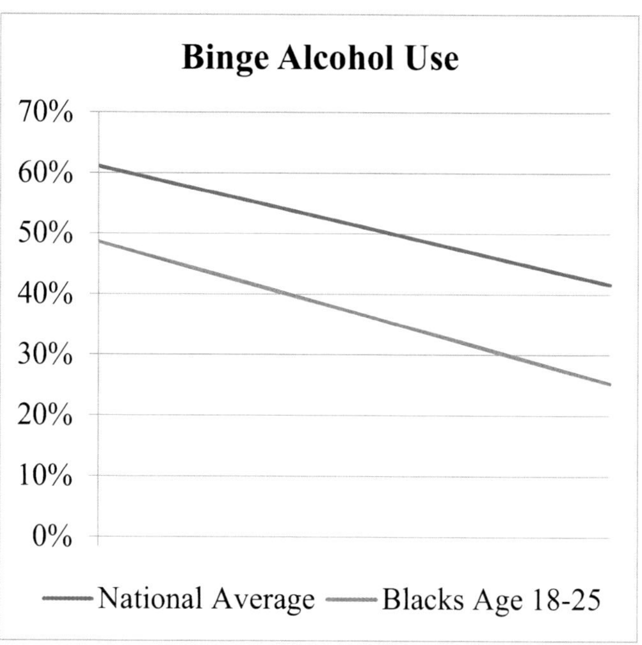

And because of this, a variety of domestic issues were also at the forefront for many of these boys and men. The incessant absence of positive role models within black communities also increases the demise among young black males. Because of poor mentorship, they are more likely to commit violent criminal acts. The shortage of male presence within homes attributes to

10. James Unnever and Samuel L. Gabbidon, *A Theory of African American Offending: Race, Racism, and Crime* (New York: Routledge, 2011), 2.

deficiency in young black males seeking to understand their own roles in the home, community, and church. Still, the young men within the study's demographic deemed to be high-risk also demonstrate a deep desire for mentoring, because just as many at-risk adolescents are looking for positive adult mirrors by whom to view themselves in a new and positive light.[11]

Additional studies propose that children reared in father-absent homes are more likely to display delinquency, experience poor masculine development, and exhibit compensatory masculine development in their teens.[12] Unable to grasp their roles and responsibilities has left many of these young men to use the bad influences of their surroundings to learn about manhood. Often times, those lessons lead to more crime, drug abuse, and becoming an unwed father. Many young black males grow up in an inner-city setting with or without father figures who cannot provide effective male mentoring because of their marginal participation in society.[13] Not fully understanding their roles further perpetuates their identity crisis, which leads them to seek out peers for validation and street recognition. Eventually, they seek status from the streets because there is no status within their homes.[14] A non-

---

11. Michael Ungar, "The Importance of Parents and Other Caregivers to the Resilience of High-risk Adolescents," *Family Process* 43, 1 (2004): 23-41.

12. Gibbs, *Young Black, and Male in America*, 7.
13. Gibbs, *Young Black, and Male in America*, 196.

14. Ibid.

existent home life further perpetuates distancing from their immediate families, communities, and loved ones. Life on the streets looks more feasible and attractive because of the promise of instant acceptance.

Certainly, it is difficult to read this information about a group that is already marginalized by society. These statistics are real. These statistics are true. But as followers of Christ, we have a responsibility to respond in righteousness. Knowing what we are facing gives us proper perspective for creating assistance for those we intend to serve. And even with despairing information, we still have a responsibility to review the statistics to change the narrative.

Chapter Four:

Influenced by the Solid Rock

So how does the church play a role in changing the narrative of the data? How does scripture help us navigate such a large task? Because our mission is led in faith, it is necessary for us to consider that close to the issues of male mentorship among young black males is the deficiency of spirituality among black males. No affiliation to God or anything religious or spiritual increases the delinquency in this group. Their moral compasses reflect a depraved mind and their lifestyle perpetuates low standards.

To be clear, religion, for them, is not viewed as a means of hope but rather a means of judgment and persecution. "Survival of the fittest" drives their yearning to live, and religion impedes their means of providing for themselves, which often leads to crime. Embracing love over rage or hate makes them appear lax and unable to protect themselves in the harsh environment of the streets. The young men pride themselves on being tough, which means that the greater the potential danger inherent in any given situation, the greater the potential proving ground for one's "bad boy" behavior.[15] Toughness, violence, and disregard for death and danger become the hallmark of survival in a world that does not respond to reasonable efforts to belong and achieve.[16]

Consequently, young black males struggle with the question, "If God is so good, why are things so bad?" The sovereignty of God has little meaning to this generation as they evaluate and engage life. Persecution and struggle push them further down the abyss, which further alienates them from a loving relationship with God. Moreover, they cannot develop spiritually because there is no relationship between them and God. They become more likely to commit crimes of all types, including those that are atrocious and violent, because their moral compass cannot differentiate between right and wrong.

Due to the lack of connectivity to God, the young men cannot identify behavioral issues, which renders them unable to modify their actions. Young black males within the scope of this project will benefit from an awareness of the Holy Spirit's guidance and influence toward spiritual maturity. The Bible describes a distinctive path for spiritual development, and it is within the context of Christianity that one's personal relationship

---

15. Edith Folb, *Running Down Some Lines: The Language and Culture of Black Teenagers* (Cambridge: MA, Harvard University Press, 1980), 42.

16. Richard C. Majors and Janet M. Billson, *Cool Pose: The Dilemma of Black Manhood in America.* (New York: Lexington Books, 1992), 34.

and identification to the person of Jesus Christ develops. In fact, Christianity as a whole is centered on a relationship with Christ. Spiritual growth from a Christian perspective is established through the context of the Bible, which as the primary witness to the teachings and witness of Jesus Christ displays the Gospel as the foundation for spiritual growth.

The Bible further sustains this truth of identification and relationship to Jesus Christ as a means for spiritual growth. When people believe in the good news of the Gospel, they are filled with the Spirit of God that enables them to engage in a lifetime of spiritual formation and growth. Acts 2:4 uses the word "filled" to denote the impartation of the Holy Spirit to the disciples in the Upper Room, which meant that the men were filled with something new that supplanted what formerly filled them. As a person is filled with the Holy Spirit, it resides and takes over the person, thus establishing new actions, deeds, and motives. The Bible also states that as a person repents of their sin and believes in the message of the Gospel, the Holy Spirit leads them into all truth while encouraging spiritual development.

Furthermore, scripture suggests that spiritual growth occurs because of God's direction and the believer inclining his or her will toward God. Scripture becomes the means that Christians use to discern the will of God that supports a more mature faith; thus, the Bible guides believers in the desire for spiritual renewal and transformation. As one develops in the faith, signs of conversion manifest through individual scripture reading and prayer. To further describe the traits of spiritual growth, the Apostle Paul gives three characteristics for the process of maturity found in Heb. 5:12-14:

> In fact, though by this time you ought to be teachers, you need someone to teach you the elementary truths of God's word all over again. You need milk, not solid food! Anyone who lives on milk, being still an infant, is not acquainted with the teaching about righteousness. But solid food is for the mature, who by constant use have trained themselves to distinguish good from evil.

Therefore, foundations for spiritual growth require an initial relationship with the Lord Jesus Christ through salvation. As one develops an initial relationship with Jesus Christ, one's eyes are opened to the reality of sin's existence and the effects of sin throughout one's experiences. Recognition of sin challenges converts to trust and depend on the person of Jesus Christ to forgive them of sin, which is essentially trusting Christ for forgiveness of sin and redemption and begins the process of developing a foundation for spiritual growth.

Establishing a relationship with Jesus Christ is essential for ratifying delinquency among young black males. By accepting Christ as Savior, one has a renewed perspective on life.

Recognizing and relating to the message of the Gospel encourages believers to remain secure in their spiritual status before God based on Jesus' labor of love. Learning to obey God and radically reorienting one's priorities assists in developing spiritual maturity and hope. The Gospel is the foundation for spiritual growth, and the power of the Holy Spirit maintains spiritual maturity through prayer and Bible reading within the context of personal and corporate spirituality in a biblical community of faith. Becoming more like Jesus is at the core of one's spiritual growth, which is an ongoing process during the Christian journey.

Spiritual growth is an essential part of the Christian experience that profoundly alters behavior in those who adhere to the Holy Spirit's direction. Spiritual growth can also be enhanced when like-minded individuals are in fellowship with one another. This is what the small group concept promotes. Reconnecting young black males to the church, their families, and society requires a communal effort from the church and positive male mentorship. What we soon realized, in our work, was a small group concept was necessary to assist the young black males into a gradual transition, as opposed to joining a local body instantly where Christian jargon and judgment is rampant. Permitting the young men to join a smaller setting allows for development that is more personal.

It is imperative that they feel accepted as opposed to feeling isolated because they do not readily accept Christian idioms. A small group setting allows the young men to establish new community among a group of their peers who are seeking the same realities. A Christian small group emulates the pack mentality that they pursued in street life but with a different purpose and plan. It is through this concept that it is believed young black males will be impacted and transformed.

Approaching young black males in a neutral setting that does not appear intimidating or judgmental is necessary to their growth. The small group concept creates a non-threatening environment and perpetuates growth. Developing the idea of small groups as a means of transitioning, mentoring, evangelizing, reconnecting, and developing people is not a new concept. Scripture too supports this perspective. The New Testament church established the concept of small groups by creating community, spiritual growth, and conscious contributions to society that conveyed the will of God in the world. For one to understand the significance of small group structure and how it benefits the transformation of young black males, one must look at the New Testament concepts of small groups, historical foundations of small groups, and the present use of small group ministries for men eighteen to twenty-five.

Some of the first signs of New Testament small group concepts come from Jesus as he began an earthly ministry, for example, when he called four fishermen in the initial moments of his ministry in Mt. 4:18-22. Christ continued to add men, totaling twelve core members. Even though he taught large numbers of people, the twelve received special instruction and care. Later in his earthly ministry, he condensed the number to an inner circle who received deeper, more personal instruction (Mt. 17:1).

Another example depicts Christ teaching in the house of Lazarus, whom scripture says he loved (Lk. 10:38-42). The concept of church within the confines of a person's home continued into the third century. Heavy persecution caused many of the homes to limit the number of believers, which further contributed to widespread small group meetings in Christ's name. Even Jesus' declaration that "where two or three are gathered together in his name," proposes a Christological presence in small gatherings of believers (Mt. 18:20). The apostle Paul further substantiates the use of small groups due to not having a standing building (Acts 20:20). His public teaching and ministry to the church at Ephesus was in the homes of the believers as opposed to a standing building. The home context of the early church perpetuated early foundations for small cell group ministry. Small groups within the local church context helped to engage believers in the word of God and developed community, while potentially experiencing the manifestation of God. By participating in small cells, people expressed their feelings regarding life and worship, and they shared their faith experiences about Christ among the faithful. The practice became a movement that evolved and spread the Gospel throughout the modern world.

The effectiveness of the early small groups that met in homes came from a quaint atmosphere. Larger church buildings in later centuries created an impersonal atmosphere that did not provide a nurturing and sharing environment in the early days. Individuals attended like consumers rather than active participants. In the smaller setting, people cared for each other and genuinely loved each other as the good news of the Gospel penetrated their hearts and minds. The environment perpetuated a warm and inviting atmosphere that encouraged sharing and deep connection among the believers.

Much of the early New Testament writings are comprised of exhortations that came from their immediate setting. Exhortations such as loving one another, observing the Lord's Supper, and proper use of the gifts of the Spirit were rooted in a family atmosphere.[17] It is from an intimate context that people gained a more profound understanding the *Missio Dei*, or mission of God, and their role as a biblical community. Early Christians enjoyed the blessing of communal worship, praise, and training that afforded them the opportunity to put their beliefs into practice. The ability to fellowship in a smaller setting produced solid relationships and unity among believers that translated into a

---

17. J. Goetzman, *Dictionary of New Testament Theology*, Vol. 2 (Grand Rapids: Regency Books, 1976), 250.

continuation of the Day of Pentecost (Acts 2:1). Everyone enjoyed the presence of Christ and his sweet communion on one accord for his divine purpose.

In essence, if the church wants to see the change that these young men so desperately need and desire, it is imperative to understand and be influenced from the model of Jesus Christ. Scripture has provided us with several examples relative to the effects of influence and the importance of community in the lives of all people. Armed with these examples and pertinent information, Bethany Church was on a mission, with the help of God, to see that change.

Chapter Five:
A Rock-Solid Approach

The first ministry responsibility I had, as a youth leader, gave me charge over forty-nine young people ranging in age up to nineteen. The pastor wanted the ministry to be the change agent in radically altering the lives of these impressionable young men and women. There was one problem: the curriculum and methods for reaching this group was based on statistics and techniques founded fifty plus years earlier. The church as a whole desired 20th century ministry using outdated materials. The day of gathering students in large rooms to discuss the Sunday school lesson had passed and the church as a whole missed the mark, because they were content putting the young people in the same teaching and relationship building models that the adults used.

It didn't take an act of nature or God to recognize we needed a "Rock Solid" approach. If we are to truly make a spiritual and social impact, the Bible must be the first source of information, while using the information, gained from cultural statistics in the previous chapter, to develop a biblical framework for reaching youth and young adults.

Here is what's imperative about this work: we can either settle in the statistics that we have been given and continue to be made aware of while ignoring biblical examples, or we can be the salt that God has called us to be. This is essentially what these young men's stories inspired me, along with those men who also serve at Bethany Church, to do. The theological material demonstrates how young black males can develop holistically and spiritually in faith communities. It also solidifies the need for a foundation in spiritual growth as a means of developing renewal and wholeness, culminating in relevant models of ministry established for that pursue spirituality. The theoretical framework examined the high incarceration rate of young black males eighteen to twenty-five and the continuum of crimes, from minor to heinous, that they committed. Incarceration of the African American male has caused several issues among males who are in the aforementioned age group.

Small groups for males eighteen to twenty-five are not prevalent within the community of faith and it was necessary that we change that at Bethany Church. There are numerous small group programs for high school students and college age students, but few gender specific programs within the African American church setting. Research showed that a community, developed primarily of their peers, tended to stimulate a better sense of hope and greater awareness of their predicament. What once divided them could now bring unity and togetherness through small group association. The void, need for, and results of small group exercises in this demographic were both thoroughly researched and practically examined.

We decided to introduce a basketball ministry called "Pass the Rock" to encourage reconnection to the church, spiritual growth, and positive contributions to society. In this program, thirty-five young black males eighteen to twenty-five participated, allowing the practical exploration of the benefits of a basketball ministry model. Participants were selected from a questionnaire on a first come, first served basis. The congregation of Bethany Church was polled to better assess the overall issue among African American males eighteen to twenty-five and the church's ability to meet the needs of this demographic was evaluated. The evaluation provided credible information concerning the congregation's awareness of the plight of the studied demographic and the church's role in and ability to minister to this group.

Yes, small group models would prove to be effective, but we also needed to determine what would capture the attention of these small groups. The reality was and is that many black males view church as boring, critical, and irrelevant; therefore, they see no significance in attending a service or gathering of God's elect. Young people engage in a nearly constant search for fresh experiences and new sources of motivation.[18] The church has not sustained their importance to this generation of Mosaics and

---

18. David Kinnaman, *Unchristian: What A New Generation Really Thinks About Christianity* (Grand Rapids: Baker Books, 2007), 23.

Busters, nor the oppressed and marginalized black male. In a sense, the black church has lost its compassion to the needs of African American young males. The lack of sensitivity to the issues of the black males within the church has caused them to begin a journey of rediscovery disjointed from the church.

Young black male's identities remain skewed and established in a corrupt society, which opposes spirituality. The ministry structure of the black church must have a biblical paradigm or premise from which to draw validity and authority. Outreach and Missional programs to this group of displaced young men must have a foundation that is relevant to the issues of today but true to the good news of the Gospel. If there is to be deliverance regarding black males, the theoretical must be developed into a pragmatic response. A coalition between church and society is essential to ensure that young black males do not remain embittered, enraged, and enslaved to the bondage of incarceration, joblessness, discrimination, and degeneracy.

Fostering a new mindset for young black males required our church to adopt smaller settings with an emphasis on each one reaching one. Peer mentoring and dialogue among this group helped them to see each other as valuable assets. Male mentorship, as a means of redirecting the behavior and attitudes developed among young black males, gave them a positive support system. Establishing a basic understanding of the fundamentals of faith in small group settings helped broaden their perspective on the church and God. These basic principles theoretically encouraged young black males to establish hope and reconnection to the church and their families.

In the history of the church, small groups have played significant roles in bringing new spiritual life. In contemporary church organizations, the small group or cell group ministry was displayed in youth groups, Sunday school, and men's and women's ministries. Some churches have used the model as a church-planting tool. Today, fellowships such as Saddleback Ministries and others have seen exceptional growth by using cell structures. Massive ministries have evolved using the cell group structure as a means of reaching individuals through community. In some church settings, small groups function as an entry point for new converts or new members. Many of the groups are no longer composed of fellowship groups for existing members, but they serve as an initial point of entry to church membership. Robert Wuthnow adds that Christian marketing publications speak of small groups as "the key to your congregation's survival," and tout them as catalysts for stability and growth.[19] The church has its share of problems and faults, but it remains the best context for transformation and spiritual growth.

---

19. Robert Wuthnow, *"I Come Away Stronger": How Small Groups Are Shaping American Religion* (Grand Rapids: Eerdmans Publishing Company, 1994), 33.

With the aforementioned in mind, a primary interpretive task of the black church that ministers to the African American male eighteen to twenty-five is to redefine their model of ministry through community. Previous chapters have outlined the obstacles, issues, and occasional heinous outcomes surrounding the young black male. By identifying the systemic issues surrounding their communities, homes, and church, it was incumbent upon Bethany Church to make radical changes to address this almost extinct group. The church universal too needs to revolutionize their methods to reach this group to avoid further decadence and disenfranchisement. Development of faith in this particular age group must be pointed and radical to be effective.

The data we found and collected afforded Bethany Church an opportunity to create a model of ministry aimed at addressing various issues concerning African American males eighteen to twenty-five who are caught in waves of societal, historical, and spiritual crises. "Pass the Rock" offered a ministry aimed at mitigating certain areas of crises in the lives of young African American males in the studied demographic. The project can be reproduced in any church or para-church setting that has access to an indoor gymnasium and willing volunteers with energy among the laity and community. While the project had limitations that were short-term in their scope and intent, the ultimate plan and scope of this project is long-term, with lasting spiritual implications in all participants. The study drew several conclusions from the statistical data obtained, primarily centering on the fact that African American males eighteen to twenty-five are in a fight for survival, and the church must not relent in its pursuit to minister and nurture this group towards spiritual wholeness.

Let's see how it was done!

Chapter Six:

Pass the Rock

What came to mind, after listening to the hopelessness of these young men, was getting them to return to the church. Getting these young men to return to a place of salvific and holistic spirituality would require a ministry model that would meet their needs. This challenge became the focus for developing a model of ministry for them. Hence, "Pass the Rock" ministry was birthed to meet the spiritual needs of young black males at Bethany Church and the surrounding community and structure, along with implementation, would prove to be everything to the participant's and program's success.

Considering a key recommendation from the pastor, the leadership team of mentors and coaches had to first answer several questions to move forward:

- *How do we create a magnetic appeal in the ministry model for this group?*
- *How do we incorporate community and small group Bible study into the model?*
- *How do we establish foundations for spiritual growth in the participants?*
- *How do we use the model to reconnect young black males to a local church?*

- *How do we encourage hope in the participants?*

After gathering the collective responses and conversations of the leadership team, it was apparent that the most appealing magnet to this demographic was sports—primarily, football and basketball were the two most popular during the dialogue. Since Bethany Church already had an indoor gym, the venue was set, and the game of basketball would be the magnet. This research proved that African Americans dominate professional basketball and young black males view athletes as role models. The allure of the sports comes from the enormous salaries that professional basketball players make and the lifestyles that their salaries afford them. Young black males in this age bracket are addicted to sports, especially basketball. The cheers of fans, whistle blowing, the competitive nature of the game, and an opportunity to showcase their talents among their peers is inviting. Thirty-six out of forty-five of the participants said that if basketball had not been provided, they would not have participated in the ministry model. Even though there is nothing salvific in basketball, one cannot disciple someone who is not present.

Mission Statement

In recognition of the great chasm that exists between the church and young African American males eighteen to twenty-five, a ministry model was developed for Bethany Church. The model was called "Pass the Rock" and it was designed to interact with the group of study by promoting reconnection to the church, spiritual growth, to encourage Bible study, and to make positive contributions to society. Creating a ministry that was relevant and effective meant establishing a mission statement focused on meeting the spiritual needs of African American males eighteen to twenty-five. The ministry would accomplish its goals through relevant Bible study, transformational mentorship, and establishing foundations for spirituality and hope.

Goals

Based on the mission statement, the following goals were created as guiding principles to maintain the overall vision and to accomplish the mission for ministering to this demographic. To adequately meet the mission, "Pass the Rock" must:

1) Provide present Jesus Christ as Lord and Savior;

2) Provide positive and spiritual role models and peers as an alternative to undesirable relationships;

3) Provide a facility for basketball as recreation and outlet for stress;

4) Provide the life skill training necessary to acquire gainful employment to make positive contributions to society;

5) Provide seminary-trained counselors as a deterrent from negative and dysfunctional decisions surrounding young African American males.

Objectives

The following objectives of "Pass The Rock" were established to meet the goals of the mission. To adequately meet the needs of African American males, they would be encouraged to learn how:

1) To have faith in Jesus Christ by developing a spiritual foundation through Bible study;

2) To work in community with others by playing on a team;

3) To choose role models and peers that could be positive influences in their lives;

4) To make positive contributions to society by displaying positive behavior and pursuing gainful employment.

Methodology

"Pass the Rock" basketball and Bible study ministry was a simple but impactful ministry model to facilitate. The following steps were comprised the methods used to administer the program:

1) Secure the recreational facility at Bethany Church once a week on Sunday evenings;

2) Select coaches and mentors (some basketball knowledge and or coaching would be necessary) that were capable of teaching;

3) Determine a biblical curriculum;

4) Enlist and enroll participants by using a questionnaire, flyers, and word of mouth;

5) Implement an assessment tool (questionnaire, exit interview) initially, and at subsequent times to monitor personal spiritual growth and development.

Establishment of Participants

From the onset, to develop an effective ministry model, the congregation of Bethany Church was polled with a simple questionnaire that sought to discover if congregants overall believed Bethany Church met the spiritual needs of African American males eighteen to twenty-five. Based on the overall congregation's assessment, the percentage of parishioners believed Bethany Church was not doing enough to enhance the spiritual awareness of young black males.

Consequently, males within the demographic of study also filled out the questionnaire. Eighty-one percent of the young men believed that Bethany Church did not have relevant ministries and resources that ministered effectively to their individual needs. As a result of their collective answers, another questionnaire was developed to be answered only by males who did not attend Bethany Church, but who lived in the community where the church was situated. Forty-five young black males within the demographic of study all responded in the same manner as the congregation. Once the data was compiled, the same groups of young men were asked if they would participate in a basketball and Bible study program. Each person was asked to give a day of preference to attend. The young men all seemed to prefer Sunday afternoons as a day to engage in the program. They were also asked to sign waivers of liability for Bethany Church and to fill out contact forms in case of emergency to be used later as contact information.

Two weeks after all the young men agreed to participate, a plea went out to the congregation soliciting all males who would like to become basketball coaches and mentors to meet at Bethany Church the following Monday night. The first meeting yielded fourteen men of a congregation that boasts a membership of 3,500 people and more than 2,000 families. At the first meeting, each person was given another questionnaire asking them about their basketball experience, coaching and mentorship experience, Bible teaching experience, membership status, job status, and families. All of the questionnaires received that night had positive responses.

The men were asked to participate in a three-month basketball and Bible study program that started at 6:00 p.m. every Sunday and ended at 10:00 p.m. Only eleven men were able to commit to a three-month program and the other three volunteered to participate once a month. Each man who committed to participate went through a four-week class on discipleship and witnessing using the curriculum, "Master Life: Developing A Rich Personal Relationship with Jesus Christ" by Avery Willis.

Upon successful completion of the four-week class, each man was coupled with another man who would be their backup coach/mentor. All the men were asked to develop mentoring relationships over the next three months with each young man within their team structure. Each team would be equally divided into five groups of eight, and any newcomers would be added to the team that had the least number of wins in the season. Enrollment for "Pass the Rock" would close the third week of play, and each newcomer would provide contact information to be called upon for the start of the next season.

After solidifying coaches and mentors, the three men who were unable to give a long-term commitment were asked to partner with the work source and obtain information on preparing for the job market. The men were also asked to give three presentations on filling out an application for a job, proper attire for a job, and what to say in a potential interview. Each presentation would take place at the beginning of the month before games and after Bible study. The following rules were established for all participants in "Pass the Rock" by the coaches and leadership teams:

1) Absolutely no fighting;

2) No cursing;

3) All coaches/mentors will be respected, or a participant could be suspended from play and/or asked not to return;

4) No Bible study, no play on that day. A person can make up Bible study at the second session after their game. If they do not make up Bible study on the day of play, they will have to sit out the following week;

5) Participants must attend one Sunday service during the three-month league play.

The week before league play began, all the participants were called and given a team number, the phone numbers of their teammates, and a coach. Rosters were generated indicating each team member and coach's names. Schedules indicating games and bye weeks for each team were prepared, and playoff brackets were made to be completed at a later date. In addition, copies of the rules and schedules were prepared for each participant.

Teachers were established last. A rotation of four teachers was established to teach the same Master life curriculum that each mentor participated in prior. The class facilitators were picked from the core of ministers at Bethany Church. All males were selected, and each had to have significant experience in teaching. A rotation of four would be used to establish two classes every Sunday night for the participants who were either on time or late, which provided teachers an opportunity to teach but limited burnout. Each week had a backup scheduled to alleviate any issues regarding teaching. The teachers taught from Master Life curriculum. Each taught the curriculum first through Bethany Church's Sunday school class in the months prior to the kick-off in order to familiarize themselves with the material.

Services and Opportunities

Other services were provided and offered to the Pass The Rock participants. During the duration of the ministry, all participants were encouraged to fellowship with Bethany Church and other local assemblies where they lived as a means of fostering relationships with the faith community. To further help the young men to realize that they were in fellowship with a biblical community, other opportunities also were extended to them. Throughout the week, practical service in areas such as weekday

Bible study, food pantry, and benevolence were offered to the participants as a means of enhancing their experience at "Pass the Rock." Locally, a social worker, who was on retainer at Bethany Church, provided appointments for biblical counseling for any participants on Monday and Tuesday evenings.

Additionally, the church office of Bethany Church provided resources for all participants Monday through Friday such as:

1) The secretarial staff of Bethany Church provided participants the location and contact information for area GED courses;

2) Printing of resumes, applications, and computer use was provided by the front office secretary;

3) Bus tokens were provided by the front office secretary for participants who were attending job interviews;

4) Assistance with editing resumes and emailing was made available;

5) Information for social health services and programs was provided.

These were all key pieces to ensuring that the program could operate at full potential. These pieces were also necessary in ensuring that not only was the program a success, but the young men it served were too. This model worked for Bethany Church and there is room for adjustments that meet the needs of the congregations that you serve. The key to the success of the program relied on the guidance of the Holy Spirit, the willingness of church leaders and participants and the *structure* of the program.

Chapter Seven:

Rocking the Boat

I hear you. *Did it actually work? What happened to the young men? How did they change?* The first day of "Pass the Rock" started May 18, 2014, with thirty-five participants attending the first evening. All eleven coaches/mentors were present as well as the first rotation of teachers. Once all the participants had arrived, the leader gave an introduction during which all coaches/mentors were acknowledged and given an opportunity to state their professions and hobbies. The young men were asked to introduce themselves and state if they attended a church, and the high school or college they attended. After introductions, the schedules and rules were distributed and reviewed, with adjustments made as needed. Once these were clear, the first Bible study class began. Chapter one of Master Life was taught and the class took approximately twenty-five minutes, after which an invitation to relationship with Christ was extended.

During the first study, one young man came to Christ! He acknowledged the call for a relationship with Christ and also said that he had never accepted Christ in his heart. This took place in front of all who attended for the purpose of creating a biblical community for him and the other participants. The small group thus setting started quite well, and the young men seemed much more interested in the session and this God of the Bible. The young man was led into a sinner's prayer, given a Bible, and his information was given to the Bethany Church membership secretary to process him as a new member. He expressed a desire to become a member of the church, so pertinent information was given to him. Everyone was asked to bow in prayer for this soul who had received Christ that night.

Once the Bible study and invitation to Christ were concluded, the young men were introduced to a deacon of the church, who was responsible for resume building and job interview preparation. The presentation highlighted the change in the culture and the expectations that interviewers have for individuals seeking employment. He also gave the young men a riveting introduction regarding attire and what various industries would be looking for from prospective employees. Some asked questions about attire, tattoos, past criminal records, and felony charges on their records. This deacon answered the questions from his experience as an employer and General Manager of a large firm. The critical question for most of the young men focused on how to get around a criminal record during the interview process. At the close of his presentation, the young men were asked to go with their teams.

The games began at 7:00 p.m. with two prospective teams playing the first game. Proceeding games were played one hour and fifteen minutes apart; the final game was played at 11:15 p.m. The last teams were asked to help clean the gym prior to leaving to encourage a sense of ownership of the ministry; every team was assigned a day to clean up during the season. For the next three months, this was the schedule for the ministry model with minimal variances on start and finish times.

Graduation

Prior to the last week of playoffs, each participant was given an exit interview, during which they were asked to fill out a questionnaire and a comment card indicating what they liked and did not like about the ministry model. Thirty-five young men filled the cards out completely and gave helpful insight regarding their involvement. Prior to the championship game, the men were asked to share something that they gained from participating in the ministry. One by one, they stood and shared testimonies of faith and challenges that they overcame as a result of participating in Pass The Rock.

After each young man shared, the coaches and mentors were asked to share their comments regarding the young men and their involvement with them. The coaches gave great insight regarding the young men and used facets of basketball as an illustration about life. Some shared testimonies that were similar to those of the young men, which helped them to relate well. Others shared stories of times during which they saw the young men mature during adversity. The clincher was listening to an older coach use the small group sessions as a means to help the young men see their teams as a community. He also made the correlation between the team and the universal community of faith. Some of the mentors discussed relationships that had been developed through the three-month process and how they would like to further those relationships.

The Bible study teachers shared how some of the young men had been challenged regarding the Master Life curriculum and some of the concepts in the guide. Modeling forgiveness and living in forgiveness seemed to be the most challenging for the young men to embrace. One teacher took the time to give a ten-minute testimony of forgiveness to help the young men see the necessity for forgiving themselves and others. Another discussed a portion of the lesson to help emphasize God's plan of redemption through forgiveness of sin.

Once everyone finished speaking, the young men were told that after the championship game there would be a small reception. At the reception, there was an award ceremony for their participation to which their families were invited. On the day of the final game and championship, certificates of participation were given to each young man by the program facilitator and leader. In the address, he covered the importance of family within the home and the significance of the church family. Participants were encouraged to embrace the value of the church and the benefits of being in the body. There was emphasis on the importance of the ministry and how it not only blessed the participants but also the facilitators.

The facilitators asked the young men to share something that they overcame or were doing new as a result of their ministry involvement. Several of the young men discussed connection to church as the new constant in their lives. Others discussed the importance of reading the Bible once a day to maintain what they have learned. There were those who reconnected to family members through forgiveness. Prior to the close of the program, one of the young men addressed his peers and asked to give the facilitators and coaches a hand of applause to acknowledge their gratitude. At the close of the event, there was a community prayer for all the participants and their families to become actively involved with a local assembly.

Participant Benefits

"Pass the Rock" provided a caring and nurturing environment in which young men were developed and their relationships with God and peers strengthened. By participating in this program, the males gained a unique perspective on God and church. Recognition of God assisted the young men in identifying the church as a place that fosters loving relationships as opposed to the general culture's view of it being a place of judgment. By using basketball as a hook, the participants enjoyed safe and significant recreation among a group of their peers. Enjoying recreation in a safe environment that nurtured and fostered positive relationships created a sense of hope.

The participants engaged in small group Bible study in an environment that encouraged questions regarding the person of Jesus Christ and the church. A culture that typically lacked hope and had a low regard for God embraced the invitation of Christ in a non-offensive way. Discovering the love of Christ through forgiveness of sin and salvation allowed the young men to experience God. All of the false and negative labels that society had placed on the young men were not allowed in the gym, but instead they were each viewed as equally valuable and worthy. The businessman, lawyer, car salesman, mechanic, and cashier were all on the same level. A sense of equality tore down barriers as the young men saw their peers and the community as a place of nurture and commonality.

Playing basketball with individuals at Bethany Church created a community of faith as the young men engaged in recreation and spiritual growth together. Viewing systemic issues of failure from the lens of their peers and mentors stimulated a desire for reconciliation in the participants. Coming face to face with their own struggles in community aided the young men in finding peace. Having a mentor to share and openly engage them from a biblical perspective regarding choices helped them to make good decisions. "Pass the Rock" ministry challenged the young men to embrace a relationship with Jesus Christ through the means of basketball while creating a deeper awareness of God.

Playing on a basketball team also built friendships, trust, and unity among those playing. Research suggested within the context of their teams, participants developed a communality that exhibited characteristics of having faith. Mutual sharing, compassion for team members, trust, celebrating together, sharing in defeat together, meeting for a common goal, learning about Christ, and overcoming challenges together were apparent. The research proved that being in a group setting with shared goals enhanced the desire to learn together in community. Individuals became transparent with their peers and mentors, which created bonds of acceptance and transformation.

It was the belief of Bethany Church and those who work in the leadership of "Pass the Rock" ministry that a personal relationship with God through Jesus Christ is imperative to successful living. They also believed that much of the systemic issues that young black males are experiencing emanates from a lack of Christian values and concepts. Research revealed congruence with these beliefs, in that eighty percent of the participants had little or no biblical foundation. In fact, for some, this was the first time that they had entered into a church setting unless it had been for a funeral. By being a part of community through basketball, it was easier to introduce a foundation for Jesus Christ to them in a non-threatening environment. The ability to ask questions and discuss openly their challenges as well as their convictions proved to be beneficial. To enhance the experience, the leadership chose a curriculum that would introduce salvation, discipleship, and foundations for spirituality. *Master Life: Developing A Rich Personal Relationship with Jesus Christ.*

A total of twenty-six new converts were confirmed and nine made recommitments to Christ in the course of three-months. The benefit of nurturing and biblical teaching in small groups was confirmation that the historical content revealed in the research section of this project was conclusive. It demonstrated that young black males are more willing to commit to reconnect to the church when they are nurtured and genuinely cared for in small group settings with a culturally attractional appeal. In addition, they learn in significantly more in non-threatening small groups, as the safe environment enhance

This also revealed the necessity of the church to engage young black males with a model that is magnetic. Jesus Christ drew large crowds because of the magnetism of his message and his ministry; the master captivated them because there was an attractional element in his methods and proclamation. No matter their background, his message incorporated every area of their lives. When he spoke to fisherman, he identified with them by discussing fishing as a means of evangelism (Matt. 4:19). Each time that Christ targeted an individual or a group, he was able to gain their attention because he was sensitive to their context while being culturally intelligent. He knew the disciples' passion and labor revolved around fishing. By incorporating their livelihood into his dialogue, he gained their attention; in essence, he used their culture as a means of identifying their felt needs for the purpose of transformation.

Small group Bible study played a significant role in establishing transformation among the demographic. In sessions that were relevant, relational, and redemptive, the young men thrived and began to desire a deeper relationship with Christ. Genuine faith experience in the young men developed as they participated in Bible study. Learning and embracing biblical truth within a small faith community that shared a common goal of remaining in relationship with Christ perpetuated genuine faith experiences leading toward spirituality. Participating in a community of faith through small groups helped the young black men to embrace corporate study, witness, and worship, all of which are essential tools for reconnecting with the church and a faith community.

Finally, mentorship played a significant role in demonstrating a model of a believer's lifestyle that exhibited positive influences in the participants' lives. The mentors displayed Christian principles and practice that were positive influences that the young black males could imitate. They fostered relationships that essentially nurtured, cared, and empowered them to maintain biblical standards to begin to overcome social, economic, and political barriers in their lives. Enlightened by their relationship with Jesus Christ, surroundings, and mindset, the young men became more aware of God mediated circumstances. Learning to manage their decisions by viewing mentors who modeled Christian lives assisted them in maintaining a biblical standard that they could attribute to the person of Jesus Christ.

Chapter Eight:

Take the Rock and Roll

We have taken time to address the issues, look at the data, grasp a proper theological perspective, understand what implementation looks like and rejoiced in the outcomes of a work committed to changing the lives of a marginalized but valued group of individuals. So, what do we do from here? Honestly, responding to the plight of African American males eighteen to twenty-five cannot be limited to a basketball program because the young men require liberation from sin. It was not enough for the ministry to be magnetic because there was a bigger need for the participants to have a foundation. The project research revealed that this demographic required a spiritual foundation that stimulated growth to maintain a positive lifestyle.

Establishing a relationship with Jesus Christ was an essential element in developing spirituality among the participants. Most of the young men exhibited a tremendous amount of guilt concerning their lifestyles and past experiences. Therefore, Pass the Rock focused on a message of salvation through Jesus Christ to reclaim thirty-five at-risk young men. The hopelessness that resides in the culture for young black males comes from a lack of hope and an unknown future. Introducing the good news of Jesus Christ and the cross of Calvary requires consistent Bible study and teaching. Allowing the young black males to engage in a relevant small group study that was geared towards relationship and fellowship with Jesus Christ promoted genuine faith.

Theoretical research outlined the issues confronting African American males eighteen to twenty-five, which aided their delinquency, hopelessness, and lack of spirituality. The negative realities that existed prior to the ministry model ceased as the young men recognized their restored relationships in Jesus Christ through reconciliation. By being empowered through salvation, redemption, reconciliation, and a faith community, they possessed the necessary tools to guard against the systemic and societal encumbrances in their lives.

Still-- adopting this ministry model means that the church can no longer maintain a traditional method for ministering to African American males eighteen to twenty-five. Establishing a model that seeks to identify with their culture and context is essential. By seeking to embrace the social differences that are inclusive of ministering to this culture means learning how to be non-judgmental. Inclusion of this group of young men is a serious responsibility of the church that cannot be avoided or overlooked. Assisting them to reach their potential academically through formal education or alternatives that help them to take part in society is critical. Using the life skills gained through workshops concerning how to fill out a job application, proper attire for interviews, and what employers are looking for out of potential candidates was of great practical benefit.

"Pass the Rock" basketball and Bible study is a model of ministry that is not stagnate but rather it is always becoming. It is a life-giving ministry that can effectively change the lives of young adult African American males. The degradation that exists in the inner city and in black faith communities of young black males is a responsibility of the church. Saving them from extinction through the means of the church is radical but necessary. It will take a total reshaping of ministry models that have grown lifeless. "Pass the Rock" offers a ministry model that embodies the biblical paradigm of Jesus Christ by being magnetic, grounded in the Word, and empowering. This ministry model is not conclusive, but it offers an alternate reality instead of the demise of young African American males in this country.

Providing a venue and atmosphere where young black males can encounter God and develop genuine faith, spirituality, and hope helps to instill biblical principles that alter dysfunctional behavior. Identifying God as their guide urges effective communication with God that encourages trust and dependence on the Holy Spirit. Being a positive contributor to society became an actual reality that the participants adopted as they embraced the elements of this ministry model. It perpetuates a new paradigm for ministering to young African American males who have been rejected by the society and culture. By making a conscious effort within the universal faith community, purpose and direction were shown to encourage restoration and wholeness among young black males.

The initial questionnaires answered by the participants suggested that they were feeling isolated from their communities, families, and the church. The invitation to the participants from the church to play basketball encouraged self-worth, hope, and reconnection to the church. Exit questionnaires identified a change in attitude regarding their feelings towards the church. More than ninety percent of the young men upgraded their initial answers on all questions to a more positive outlook on self, church, peers, and spirituality.

The leadership team needed a measuring tool to appropriately identify any changes in the participants' spirituality. I'm suggesting that there were many tools available online, in Christian bookstores, and in clinical counseling resources. Some were too exhaustive and may have confused the young men. But to effectively measure the spiritual growth of young black males, a spiritual assessment tool was selected called "Belief in Personal Control Scale," or BPCS, created by Joy L. Berrenberg, which essentially was designed to measure self-perception of personal control.[20]

The BPCS uses forty-five questions that measure three areas of personal control—internal, external, and God-mediated. A

20. Joy L. Berrenberg, "The Belief in Personal Control Scale: A Measure of God-mediated and Exaggerated Control," *Journal of Personality Assessment* (1987): 51.

person will either be labeled an external controlled person (ExtC), exaggerated controlled person (ExagC), or God-mediated person (GM) during the test. A test indicating (ExtC) means a person believes his or her outcomes are self-initiated (internally) or produced by other source (externality). A score suggesting a person is a (ExagC) means they hold an extreme or unrealistic belief in their self for control. Finally, God-mediated (GM) means a person believes that God can be solicited for help concerning their outcome. The God-mediated dimension of the test evaluates those who feel that God is controlling their outcome as opposed to those who believe they have no control. Berrenberg states that a higher score of (ExtC) indicates a person perceives more internal control, a person with high (ExagC) scores indicates an exaggerated belief in their own control, and high scores of (GM) means a person has virtually no belief that God is in control.[21]

Using this tool, several sample tests were distributed to students in the project's demographic who were active members of the ministries at Bethany Church. A total of 169 males and 235 females were tested, and of this group, forty-eight were seminarians and thirty-four were psychology students; the remaining were undergraduate students. A total of 320 undergraduates had high scores in general external control (68.91) and exaggerated internal control (55.57). Their God-mediated control was at 28.27. The research from the test provided

21. Berrenberg, "The Belief in Personal Control Scale," 51.

significant data for how young adults feel regarding issues of spirituality, God, and self-control. With this information, all the young black males took the BPCS test prior to entering the program. Out of forty-five applicants, the scores were 81.37 for general external control, 72.57 for exaggerated internal control, and for God-mediated control, they scored 14.27 collectively. Since the project was initially designed to meet the needs of this marginalized group who had low spirituality and control in life, this questionnaire met the needs of evaluating the young men (see Figure 5).

The questionnaire measured self-control, which validated the statistical data revealed in the theoretical research, which identified the need for self-control in this group to limit delinquency and crime. After engaging in the three-month ministry, each young man took the test again, and all thirty-five men increased in their ability to demonstrate self-control, spiritual awareness, and hope. All of the participants answered the questions post-project significantly different than pre-project, by indicating that they were more inclined to be controlled by God "almost always" as opposed to "rarely" or "never." The biblical research asserted that spiritual growth in the Christian experience generally is evidenced by an increase in self-control. Indications of one's spiritual control is a sign of being led by the Holy Spirit, according to Gal. 5:22-23.

Figure 5. BCPS Scores Pre-Study and Control Group

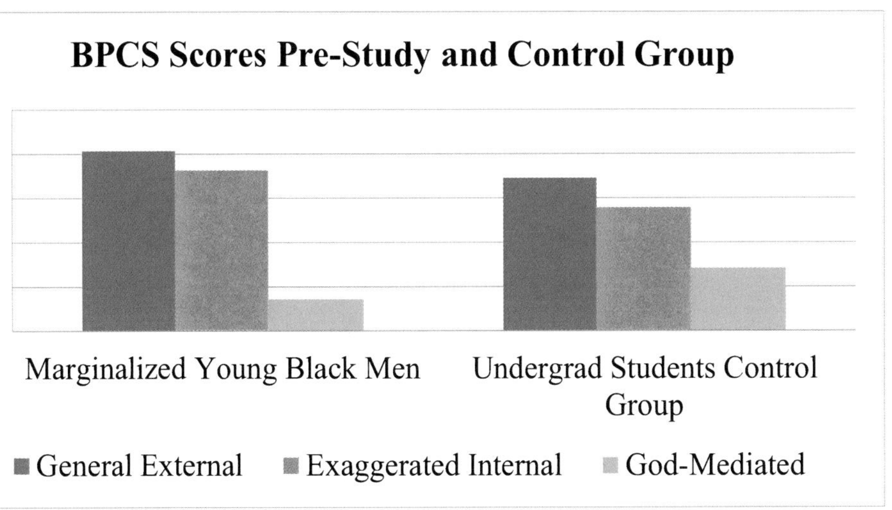

Evidence of the young men exhibiting the fruit of the Spirit was evident in their basketball games in the second month and during Bible study. Several of the young men admitted to their mentors and coaches that they no longer reacted to issues in their lives impulsively but were applying the principles taught in *Masterlife: Developing A Rich Personal Relationship with Jesus Christ*—another resource we found useful for this ministry model. Statements such as these were prevalent among the group of thirty-five, which indicated and displayed spiritual growth among the participants.

Lack of male mentorship was a major factor in the young men making choices that were detrimental to their futures. Theoretical research qualified this statement because it adequately identified national statistics within the black community and how the lack of role models in African American males eighteen to twenty-five have significantly hindered their progress socially, which contributes to their acts of violence and helplessness. By being involved in a small community or small group structure, however, they received much needed nurturing but also much needed mentoring from their coaches, who did an exceptional job by conducting practices, answering questions, identifying with the young men, and being a voice of reason.

Mentoring the young men on the basketball court created relationships that removed barriers between the church, mentors, and this demographic. As the weeks passed, the relationships grew as each mentor shared life stories with their teams during debriefings and Bible study. The mentors' personal stories regarding times of delinquency, struggle, pain, and turmoil assisted in creating venues for storytelling.

Since the theoretical, historical, and biblical research established that the young men were hopeless due to several social and spiritual issues stated in the research chapter, it was necessary to create a resource within the model that encouraged hope, while enabling the participants to make positive contributions to society. The leadership team recognized that a lack of hope often is a major factor keeping young black males from moving forward in society. Based on the evidence provided in the research chapter, hopelessness leads to criminal mischief, delinquency, and illicit drug use, all of which are signs of low morality and lack of hope.

To maintain a continuous pattern for growth, the young men needed to know that their mentors had experienced or knew their pain. Transparency from the mentors was a necessary function for the young men to share their stories in turn. It was during these times that each mentor had opportunities to exhibit the fruit of the Spirit as a demonstration for the young men to see manifested before them.

Consider resources that may be in your area too. There are nationwide resources that provide mentorship to young men, with local sub-groups, such as YBM Leadership Alliance, Big Brothers, My Brother's Keeper and the YMCA. Local organizations that exist in Texas such as The Emerging 100, Local Youth Sports Leagues and Boys to Men-Texas may exist in different entities or organizations near you. Even if a neighboring congregation has a local Boy Scouts of America program or a Boy's Rights of Passage program, they could be willing to share their insights with you to help you establish your own.

Most of the participants had either extensive or moderate criminal backgrounds during their late teens to early twenties. The application process revealed that twenty-one of the thirty-five participants indicated such. Many stated that their criminal records were impeding their ability to find gainful employment or provide for their families. To adequately encourage hope, the leadership team sought to add a component that would deal with their concern for a job. It was necessary to implement a process for encouraging hope in the young men who participated in the ministry.

The individuals were introduced to three seminars that taught proper attire for job interviews, filling out applications, and interviewing skills. A local business owner and professional shared experience from years of reviewing applications. The application process also solidified the need for this component as a means of establishing hope in the young men. Several applicants indicated on their initial application for "Pass the Rock" that they were looking for jobs, and at the launching of the basketball ministry several inquired if any of the mentors could help in the process. Allowing the participants to receive basic training and resources for securing a job established a sense of pride and hope. At least five of the thirty-five young men gave testimonials saying they received new jobs using the skills gained at the seminars. Research revealed that a lack of resources impedes the progress of young black males, but by allowing them to use the church office for emailing applications, creating resumes, and copies, it established hope.

Theoretical research established that young black males who do not have a job or education are more likely to commit violent crimes. To affect change in this area, the ministry incorporated a resource tool through the office of Bethany Church that provided information on area GED courses. Four of the participants indicated that they desired GED information from the church, and one followed through with attending classes. As of this report, he graduated with a GED and was working at a local Home Depot.

In the third and final month of the ministry, the participants were given the original questionnaire again to ensure that all the data was consistent, but which this time was used to measure spiritual growth. Each of the young black males filled out the BPCS again, and the numbers increased by ten percent for God-mediated control. The increase brought the participants within four percent of the average for 320 Christian undergraduates who took the test at Bethany Church in the same category. General external control decreased by fifteen percent and exaggerated internal control decreased by nine percent (see Figure 6).

The research conducted from the questionnaire and three months of involvement in a consistent ministry stimulated spirituality, reconnection to the church, and a relationship with God for the young black males. The changes were evidenced by participants who sought job opportunities, and one by using the resources of the church to obtain a GED. Fourteen young men visited Bethany Church and three joined the ministry as new members. As of this report, three are still active members and the other eleven are still visiting.

Figure 6. BCPS Scores Pre- and Post-Study

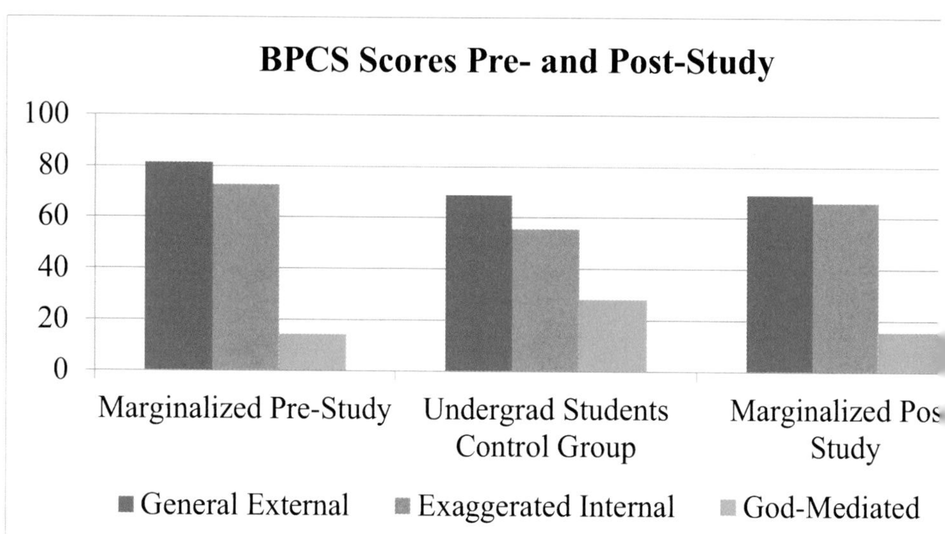

BPCS test results also proved that the level of spirituality increased enough, along with a decrease in reliance on self, to view beginning stages of transformation and discipleship from the young men who were participants of Pass the Rock. The data from Pass the Rock also documented new converts as a result of mentorship and relevant Bible study. Six of the mentors as of this report maintain relationships with the young men from the ministry for continuous mentorship. Weekly, the leadership had to turn away potential participants due to word of mouth referrals from those who attended. The magnetism of the ministry created a hunger for Bible study, basketball, resources, and connectivity. Hope was exhibited in the participants' consistent attendance and desire to maintain the ministry beyond its expiration date.

Ultimately, our goal was to commit to change. We wanted to see the church as a part of the change we so desperately sought for these young men. The task of the ministry is to provide a model for African American males eighteen to twenty-five that promoted reconnection to the church, spirituality, hope, and positive contributions to society. This model has the capability of be applied anywhere at-risk youth are present. It is my hope that you see how this work highlights how young black males are in a desperate struggle for survival and that the church must remain diligent as it seeks new and radical ways to successfully confront their demise.

Pass the Rock!

Lesson Sample

Masterlife: Developing A Rich Personal Relationship with The Master
Brown, Sherrie; Willis, Avery (1998-07-01). Masterlife B&H Publishing Group. Kindle Edition.

Chapter 1 ABIDING IN CHRIST

Jesus called His disciples to "come, follow me" (Matt. 4: 19).

More than anything else, Jesus wanted to spend time with His disciples. He knew that being with Him in all kinds of situations would equip the disciples to do that for which He had chosen them. They soon learned the truth of Jesus' declaration, "I am the vine; you are the branches. If a man remains in me and I in him, he will bear much fruit; apart from me you can do nothing" (John 15: 5). A disciple is one who follows Jesus, learns from Him, and obeys Him as Lord. God loves you and wants to have fellowship with you. Your remaining in Him is of utmost importance to God. His plans for you include spending time with Him. Only by staying in communion with Him can you be and do all for which He called you. A disciple must deny himself (Luke 9: 23) and abide in Christ (John 15: 5). The empty circle at the center of the Disciple's Cross represents your life. It pictures denying all of self and letting Christ fill the entire circle as you focus on Him. He is to have priority in everything. Life in Christ is Christ living in you. This does not mean that you lose your identity but you lose your self-centeredness. John the Baptist said, "He must become greater; I must become less" (see Matt. 3: 11). For Christ to increase does not depend on "trying" to deny self but on realizing, understanding, and accepting the lordship of Christ. When you fall in love with Jesus so that He becomes the number one priority in your life, "self" will begin to diminish as Christ Himself gives you the strength to obey everything He has commanded.

Spending Time with the Master

The primary motivation for spending time with the Master is so that your fellowship with Him grows deeper. For a child, love is spelled T-I-M-E. God gave you twenty-four hours a day. As His child, what portion of the day do you think He wants to spend with you? All of it! He said, “Surely I will be with you always, to the very end of the age” (Matt. 28: 20). He is with you every waking and sleeping hour. Spending time with the Master is not a question of God's making time for you but of your making time for Him. Wanting to communicate with someone you love is natural. When you love people, you want to spend time with them and get to know them more and more. You do not want to be separated from them. When you go for a while without seeing or talking to them, you no longer feel as close. You fail to share experiences, you lose intimacy, and you feel as if you are drifting apart. You long to connect with them once again. When you are a child of God, you have the same deep desire for fellowship with your heavenly Father. We love God as a response to His love (1 John 4: 19). You know that He loves you because He sent His Son to die for you. Failing to return God's love does not influence the way He feels about you. But your love for Him diminishes and grows stale if you do not have the nourishment of daily fellowship with Him.

A daily time together is important so you and the Father can enjoy the close relationship made possible by Jesus' sacrifice. Paul summed up what it means to fellowship with God when he wrote to the Philippians: [My determined purpose is] that I may know Him— that I may progressively become more deeply and intimately acquainted with Him, perceiving and recognizing and understanding [the wonders of His person] more strongly and more clearly. And that I may in that same way come to know the power outflowing from His resurrection [which it exerts over believers]; and that I may so share His sufferings as to be continually transformed [in spirit into His likeness even] to His death (Phil 3: 10, AMP). An Appointment with God As a young adult, I began trying to have a “quiet time,” a time set apart for the Lord. I read about Christians who got up at 4: 00 A.M. to read the Bible and pray for an hour or two before breakfast. I tried to do that, but I could not be consistent. Following that schedule for a day or two, I would be so tired that I could not get up and I would promise myself that I would try again the next day. I felt guilty because I was not consistent. I almost endangered my health before I realized that the Christians, I was reading about were going to bed at 8: 00 or 9: 00 P.M. while I was going to bed at 1: 00 or 2: 00 AM.

Then I read a tract that emphasized spending seven minutes a day with God. It stressed consistency and suggested a simple plan to achieve that goal. I decided no matter what the circumstances, I could spend seven minutes with God every morning. Of course, I soon realized seven minutes was not enough and continually set the alarm earlier to have enough time with the Lord. I learned a quiet time is more than a mere habit. It was an appointment at the beginning of the day with Jesus Christ, the center of my life. A daily quiet time helps develop your relationship with Christ. In this intimate time, He speaks with you through His Word, and you speak with Him through prayer. As you bring your needs before Him, He provides direction and guidance for your daily decisions and helps you to bear fruit for Him. If you are to have a personal, ongoing relationship with Christ, you must hear Him. The Word of God is the primary way to hear Him. Your time with Him and in His Word ensures that you have a time every day to get your orders from headquarters.

HOW TO DEVELOP A QUIET TIME

1. If you are not already doing so, find a regular time to spend with God each day that fits your schedule. Having that time in the morning begins the day with a recognition of your dependence on God and His all-sufficiency. A quiet time should be the first priority of the day. Spending time with God gives you an opportunity to yield your will to Him and consciously dedicate the day to His glory.

2. Prepare the night before. If your quiet time is in the morning, set your alarm. If it is difficult for you to wake up, plan to exercise, bathe, dress, and eat before your quiet time. Select a place where you can be alone. "But when you pray, go into your room, close the door, and pray to your Father, who is

unseen. Then your Father, who sees what is done in secret, will reward you" (Matt. 6: 6). You will find that you can concentrate best when you have an established place away from noise, distractions, and other people. Wherever you choose, make sure it is a place where you can focus on the One to whom you are praying. Gather materials, such as your Bible, notebook, and a pen or pencil, and put them in the place you selected so you will not waste time in the morning.

3. Develop a plan. Unless you consciously follow a pattern for your quirt time, you may get off track or your mind may wander. Pray for guidance. During your time with the Lord, you may want to include any number of these elements: prayer, Bible reading or study, memorizing Scripture, quietly waiting on Him worship and intercession.

4. Follow a systematic plan for your Scripture reading. For example, you may read from one of the gospels as well as another book of the Bible so that you can see Christ live out what the Scripture is teaching. You may choose to lead through the Bible a chapter a day or choose one psalm, one proverb, and one chapter of the Old or New Testament each day.
5. Allow enough time to read His word reflectively. Do not try to lead so much Scripture at one time that you cannot meditate on its meaning and let God speak directly to you and your situation. Meeting God is even more important. He created you with a capacity for fellowship with Him, and He saved you to bring about that fellowship.

My personal procedure is to kneel first in prayer and renew my relationship with God after the night's rest. Often, I incorporate adoration/ worship, confession of sin, thanksgiving, and supplication (putting my requests before God). After having fellowship with God, I sit or kneel and read Scripture. I usually read a chapter a day as I read consecutively through a book of the Bible. When I have finished, I summarize in my journal what God said to me and my response to Him. Writing each day "What God Said to Me" and "What I Said to God" helps me clarify what I have read and learned, and it becomes much easier to live out that

Word. Finally, I pray for those requests on my prayer list and anything else God leads me to pray about. Being Led by the Spirit of what God says to you through His Word. Your journal will become a living testimony to your relationship.

Pray in response to the Scriptures you have read. As you pray, use various components of prayer. Using the acronym A-C-T-S— adoration, confession, thanksgiving, supplication— helps you remember the components.

You should develop your own procedure. Choose what is helpful and manageable within the time you have. The important thing is to have a plan, so you do not waste this precious time with the Lord wondering what to do or wasting time "getting started "
Be persistent until you are consistent. Strive for consistency rather than length of time spent. Try to have a few minutes of quiet time every day rather than long devotional periods every other day.

Expect interruptions. Satan tries to prevent you from spending time with God. He fears even the weakest Christians who are on their knees. Plan around interruptions rather than being frustrated by them.
Focus on the person you are meeting rather than on the habit of having the quiet time. If the president of the United States was scheduled at your house at 6: 00 A.M. tomorrow, would you be ready? Of course.

Meeting God is even more important. He created you with a capacity for fellowship with Him, and He saved you to bring about that fellowship. My personal procedure is to kneel first in prayer and renew my relationship with God after the night's rest. Often, I incorporate adoration/ worship, confession of sin, thanksgiving, and supplication (putting my requests before God). After having fellowship with God, I sit or kneel and read Scripture. I usually read a chapter a day as I read consecutively through a book of the Bible. When I have finished, I summarize in my journal what God said to me and my response to Him. Writing each day "What God Said to Me" and "What I Said to God" helps me clarify what I have read and learned, and it becomes much easier to live out that

Word. Finally, I pray for those requests on my prayer list and anything else God leads me to pray about.

Being Led by the Spirit

Once you have established a daily quiet time, begin working on being led constantly by the Spirit. If you receive and meditate on Scripture daily, you will be aware of Him and His thoughts. He has constant access to you when you remain in His Word. You have constant access to Him by praying without ceasing. Imagine a husband and wife or two close friends taking a Sunday drive through the countryside. They do not have to talk constantly to enjoy each other's company. Even if others are along, they are aware of that special person's presence. Likewise, as you go through your day with the Lord, you can have conversations about what is important to you and to Him. As you grow in maturity, you will spend more and more time with the Father, just as Jesus did, and your knowledge of Him and your intimacy with Him will deepen. You will experience the fruit of abiding in Christ. Connie Baldwin, a schoolteacher in Virginia, gets up at 5: 30 each morning to have her quiet time. She says this helps her be more like Christ throughout the day as she works with children.

She also notices it helps her prepare for her job. “Getting up at 5: 30 for me is quite a feat because I'm not a morning person,” she claims, “but I know that God has given me the strength and determination to get up early to spend that time with Him. I know when I get to heaven, I'll never say, 'I wish I had slept more.' I'll say, 'I'm so glad I got up and spent time with my Lord!'” Enabling sinful people to commune with God cost Him His only Son. Yet God was willing to pay that price to have a relationship with you. Part of your life in Christ is daily communication with the Father. Are you willing to pay the price of a few minutes a day to have Christ live more fully in you and reveal to you the fullness of the Father? If you do so, you will experience the endless wisdom of God. In the next chapter you will see how to keep that Word rooted in your life so that the Holy Spirit can personally apply it to each particular instance of your life.

Questions for Meditation and Discussion

1. What are the best reasons for developing a consistent quiet time with God every day?
2. Are there changes you should make to help you establish a daily quiet time?
3. What element in this chapter could you add to your current plan for your time with the Lord?
4. Is your life characterized by love for the Lord, obedience to His Word, and demonstration of His character?
5. What price are you willing to pay to have Christ live more fully in you?

Bibliography

Berrenberg, Joy L. “The Belief in Personal Control Scale: A Measure of God-mediated and Exaggerated Control.” *Journal of Personality Assessment* (1987): 51.

Brown, Sherrie; Willis, Avery (1998-07-01). Masterlife B&H Publishing Group. Kindle Edition.

Cooper, Alexia. “Homicide Trends in the United States, 1980-2008.” National Criminal Justice Reference Service (Nov. 1, 2011). Accessed May 20, 2015, http://ncjrs.gov/

Folb, Edith. *Running Down Some Lines: The Language and Culture of Black Teenagers*. Cambridge: MA, Harvard University Press, 1980.

Gibbs, Jewelle Taylor. *Young Black and Male In America.* Westport: Auburn House Publishing, 1988.

Goetzman, J. *Dictionary of New Testament Theology*, vol. 2. Grand Rapids: Regency Books, 1976.

Kinnaman, David. *Unchristian: What A New Generation Really Thinks About Christianity*. Grand Rapids: Baker Books, 2007.

Klineberg, Stephen L., Jie Wu, and Kiara Douds. *The 2012 Houston Education Survey: Public Perceptions in a Critical Time.* Houston: Kinder Institute for Urban Research, 2013.

Majors, Richard C., and Janet M. Billson. *Cool Pose: The Dilemma of Black Manhood in America.* New York: Lexington Books, 1992.

Olson, Lise. "Give 'Em Hell: Resistance against Racist Oppression in the United States." Reducing the Racial Disparities in Incarceration. *Word Press* Blog (September 2007). Accessed Oct. 11, 2014, http://antiracistresistance.wordpress.com/reducing-racial-disparities-in-incarceration/

Ungar, Michael. "The Importance of Parents and Other Caregivers to the Resilience of High-risk Adolescents." *Family Process* 43, 1 (2004): 23-41.

United States Department of Labor. "Employment and Unemployment Among Youth Summary." *Economic News Release* (Aug. 13, 2014). Accessed May 26, 2015, http://www.bls.gov/news.release/youth.nr0.htm.

Unnever, James, and Samuel L. Gabbidon. *A Theory of African American Offending: Race, Racism, and Crime*. New York: Routledge, 2011.

About the Author

In September 2017, Dr. Andre J. Lewis succeeded Dr. T.R. Williams Sr., Pastor Emeritus as Senior Pastor of New Faith Church, Houston, Texas.

Born in St. Thomas Virgin Island, Rev. Lewis was reared in Boston, Massachusetts by his mother, Angela Lewis but calls Houston, Texas home. He graduated from Bellaire High School in Houston ISD and earned a B.S. in Christian Leadership from the College of Biblical Studies; a Master of Divinity and Doctor of Ministry from the Houston Graduate School of Theology, where he was recognized for outstanding achievement and excellence in urban ministry. He is a proud member of Alpha Phi Alpha Fraternity.

Rev. Lewis and his wife Kimberly, through their heritage of love, are the proud parents of four children: Andre, Ashlee, A

Pastor Lewis has served as Chaplain for Harris County Sheriff's department; Constable Precinct 7; Hightower High School (Ft. Bend ISD); Madison High School (Houston ISD); Princeton Youth Ministry Review Counsel and the Fellowship of Christian Athletes as well as community liaison for HISD South District. Currently serves as Houston Graduate School of Theology Board Member.

Dr. Lewis has lectured at Princeton Seminary for the African American Preachers Association, National Baptist Convention USA, Reload Houston, United Youth Workers Institute and has written articles for the Princeton Youth Ministry and Youth Specialties.

In addition to lecturing he has facilitated leadership trainings, symposiums and workshops for McDonald Black owners Association, other small businesses and churches worldwide.

His Christian outreach ministry has allowed him to travel across the United States, Peru, Mexico and Jamaica to share the Gospel message, build homes, develop churches and train leaders in church leadership.

Dr. Lewis believes in strong outreach programs that help frame families and the youths of tomorrow. He works in close partnership with community activist, neighborhood civic clubs, and business owners to help create a productive environment that enriches the lives of the community abroad. The key focus in his services remain essentially based on learning the word of God and making it a part of daily living and to praise and worship our Lord and Savior, Jesus Christ!

Made in the USA
Middletown, DE
17 May 2020

95175574R00058